ABC

Letter Learning Beginning Sound Coloring and Writing

This set has 26 alphabet A-Z coloring pages . Each page has an upper and lowercase letter . And each page has 4-6 objects that kid can choose the letter starting with the same letter on each page.

By Sarah Oan

Name..

Write letter A

A

A

a

Color the pictures start with letter A

Write letter B

B

B

b

Color the pictures start with letter B

Write letter C

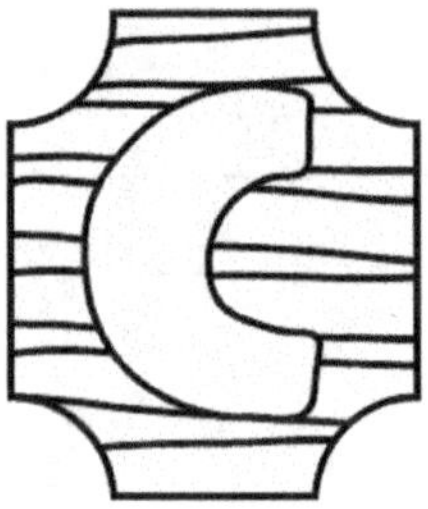

C

c

Color the pictures start with letter C

Name...

Write letter D

D

d

Color the pictures start with letter D

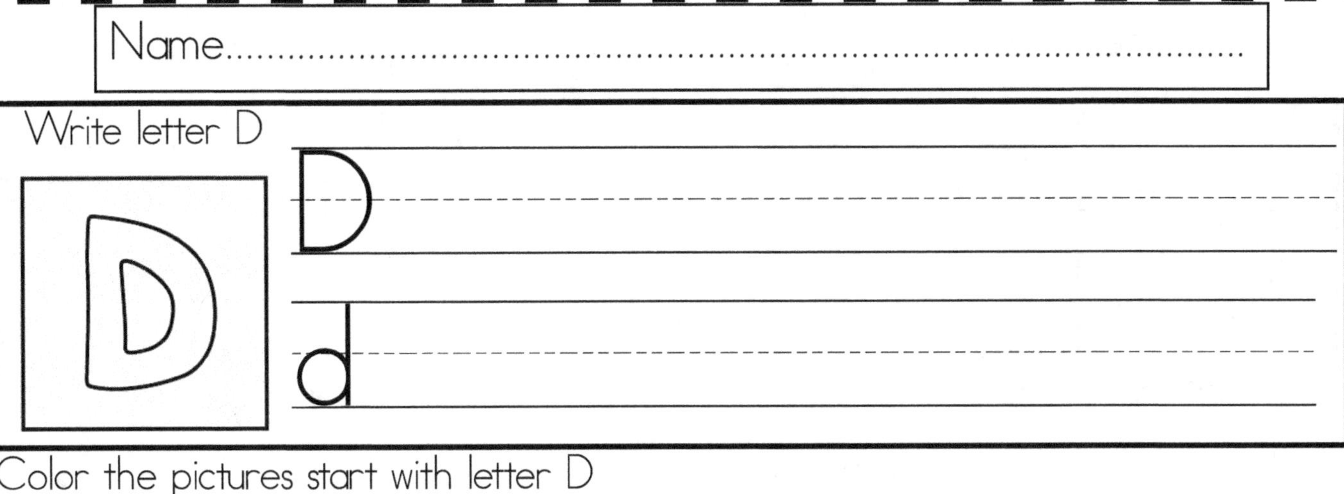

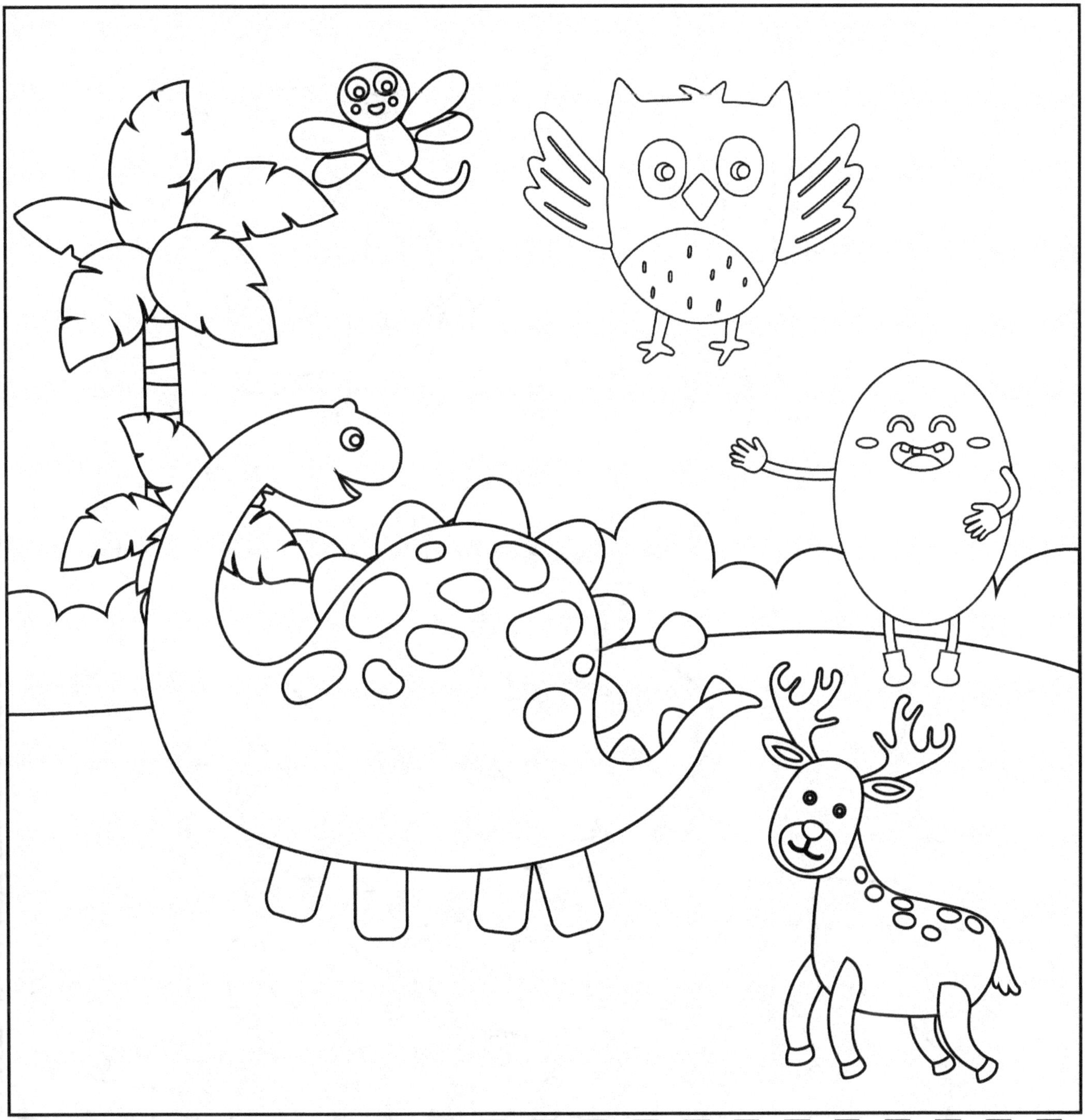

Write letter E

E

e

Color the pictures start with letter E

Name..

Write letter F

F

f

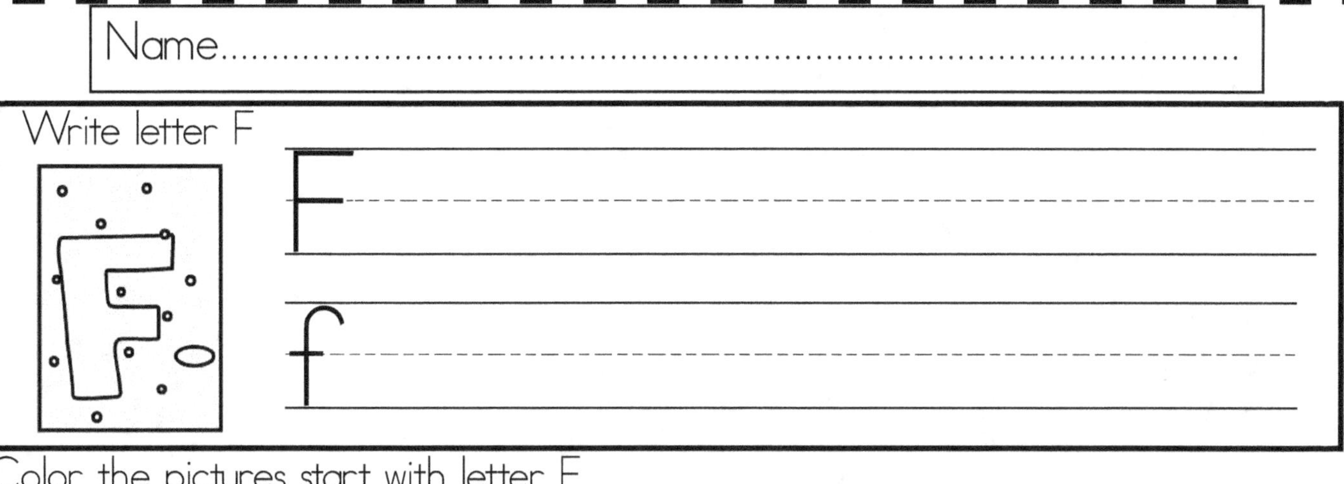

Color the pictures start with letter F

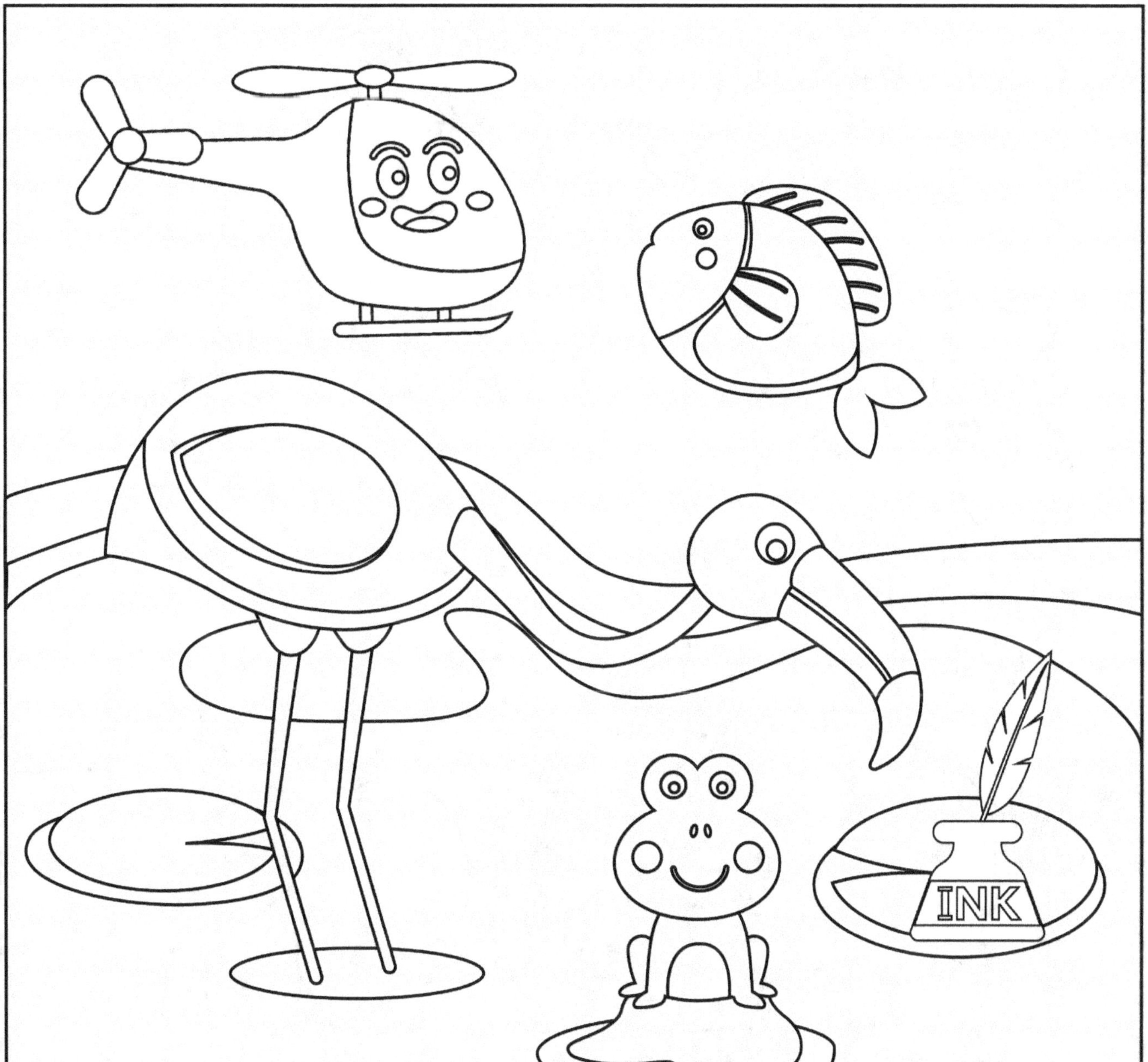

Write letter G

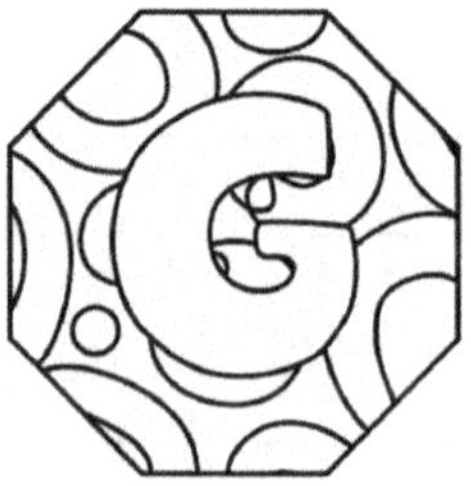

G

g

Color the pictures start with letter G

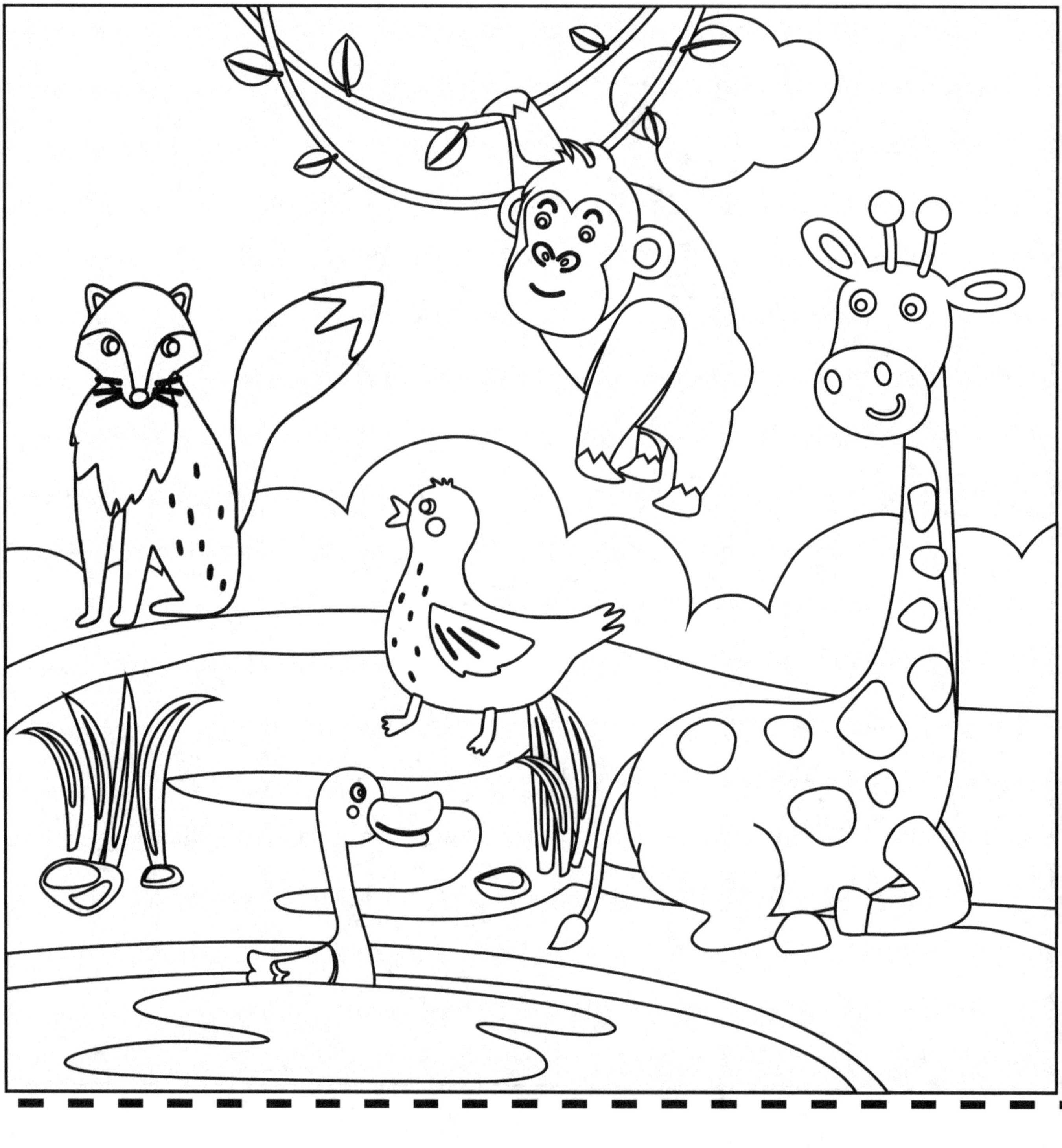

Name..

Write letter H

H

h

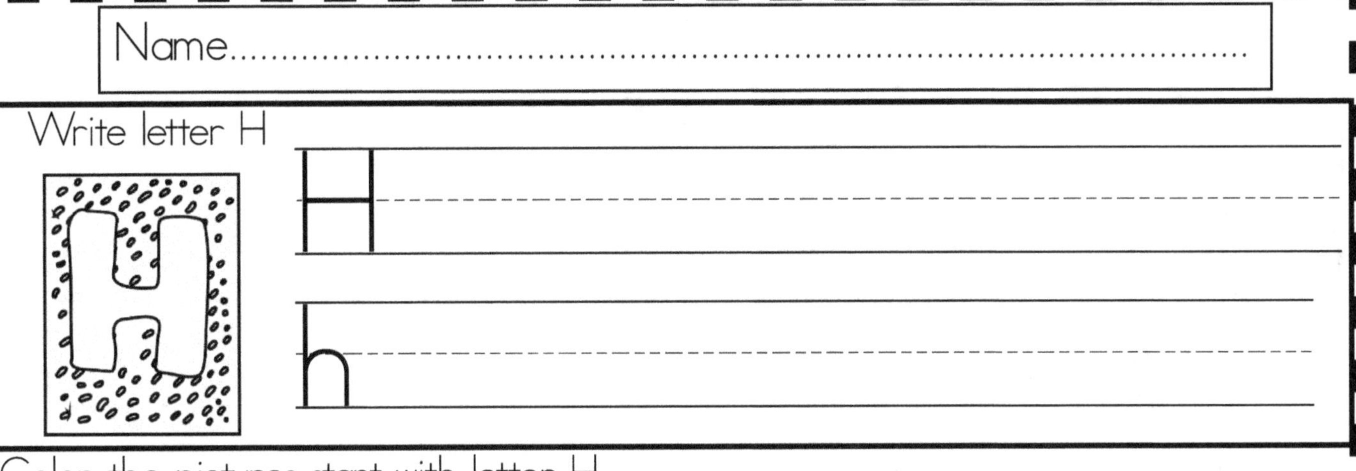

Color the pictures start with letter H

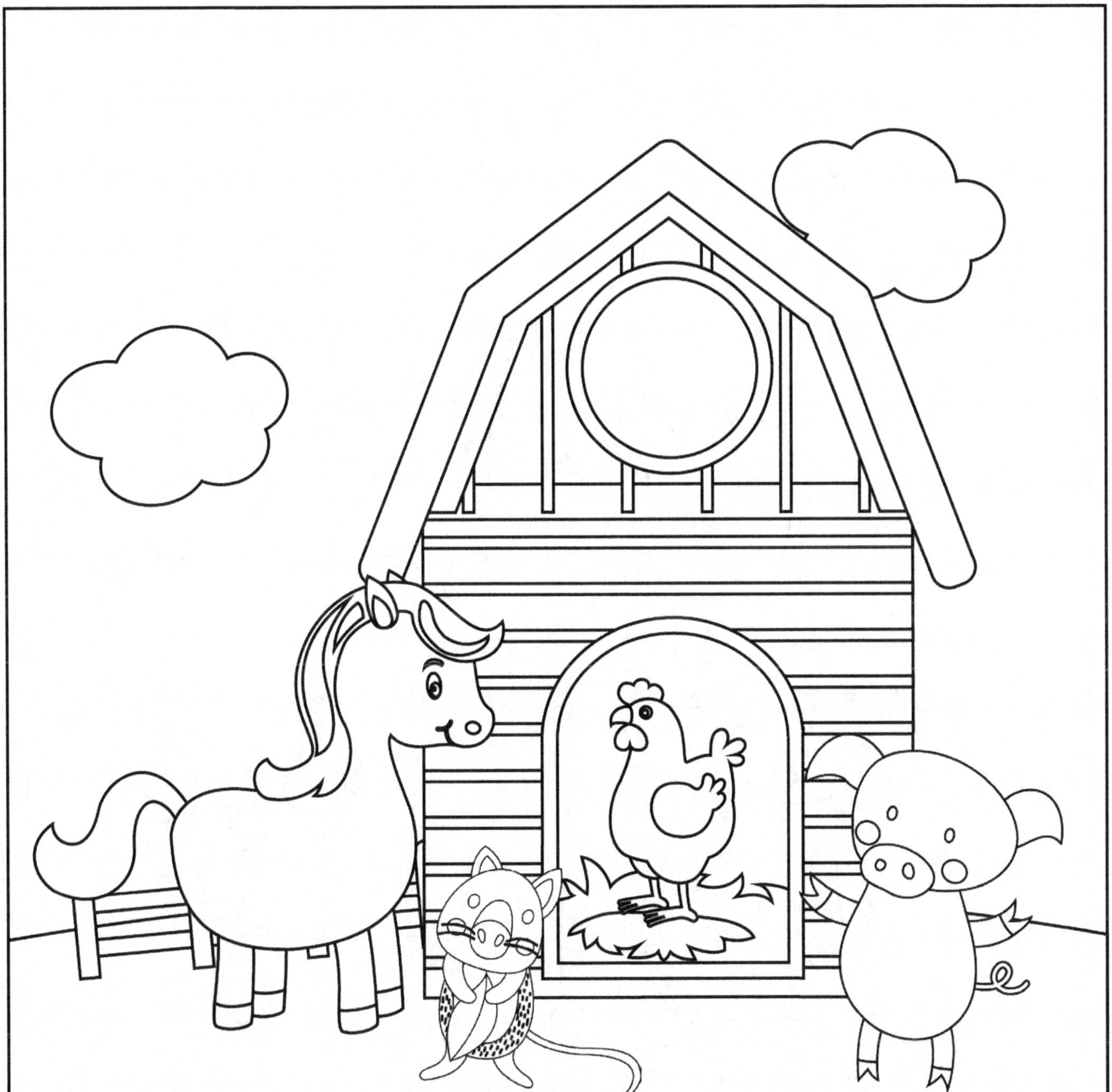

Write letter I

I

i

Color the pictures start with letter I

Name...

Write letter J

J

j

Color the pictures start with letter J

Write letter K

K

Color the pictures start with letter K

Write letter L

Color the pictures start with letter L

Write letter M

M

m

Color the pictures start with letter M

Write letter N

N

N

n

Color the pictures start with letter N

Name...

Write letter O

Color the pictures start with letter O

Name...

Write letter P

P

p

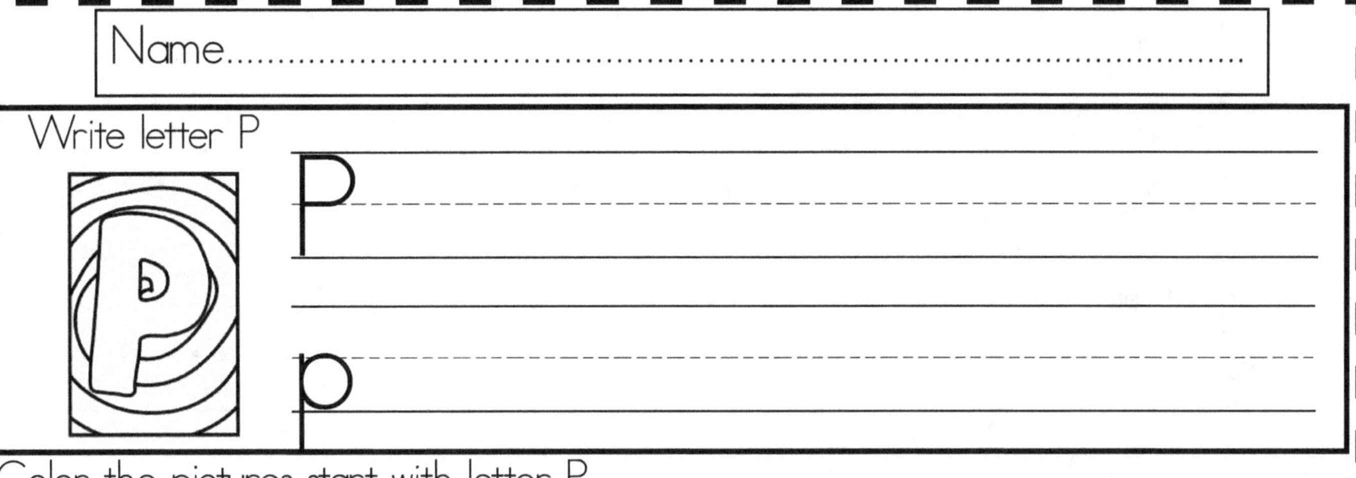

Color the pictures start with letter P

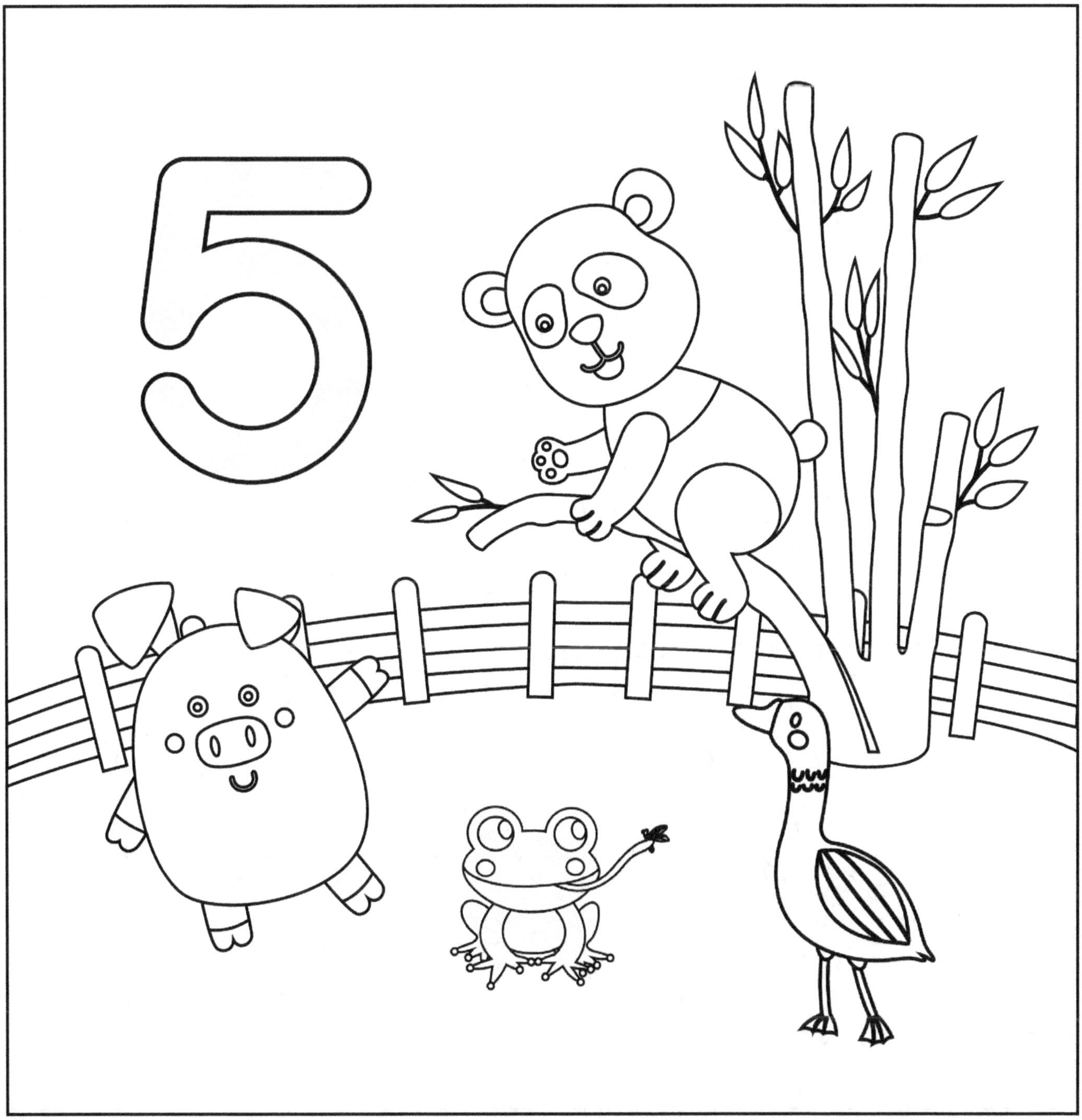

Write letter Q

Q

q

Color the pictures start with letter Q

Write letter R

R

R

r

Color the pictures start with letter R

Write letter S

S

s

Color the pictures start with letter S

Write letter T

T

t

Color the pictures start with letter T

Write letter U

U

U

U

Color the pictures start with letter U

Write letter V

V

V

Color the pictures start with letter V

Write letter W

W

W

W

Color the pictures start with letter W

Write letter X

X

X

Color the pictures start with letter X

Name..

Write letter Y

Y

Y

y

Color the pictures start with letter Y

Write letter Z

Z

Z

Z

Color the pictures start with letter Z